Copyright ©2025 by Christopher T. Saitta

Cover and back cover design by Chris Saitta. All images copyright Joseph V. Saitta and Patricia L. Saitta, except "Raven in flight on background of red rocks" © Sergey Ryzhkov, stock.adobe.com, and "Roman military dagger on white background" © jmaxstudio, stock.adobe.com.

All rights reserved.

No portion of this book may be reproduced in any form without written permission from the publisher or author, except as permitted by U.S. copyright law.

Contents

Dedication		VIII
Preface		IX
Poems of Ancient Rome and Greece		
1.	Ancient Roman Coin	3
2.	Sunset Whispers to Itself	4
3.	Egyptian Bird	5
4.	The Sumerian Goddess Grows Old	6
5.	Heart of Giza	7
6.	Babel Sighs in Ruin	8
7.	Winged Seeds of Babylon	9
8.	My Love Looks Too Far into Me	11
9.	Undercurrent	12
10.	Love Is a Phoenician Breeze	13
11.	The Desert Is Not a Grave	14
12.	Sea of the Parthenon	16
13.	The Histories	17

14.	Summer War of Youth	18
15.	Heroic	20
16.	Omens of the Oracle	22
17.	Apollo of Wolves	23
18.	Oblivion Conquers Us	25
19.	Love Lost in Every Sky	27
20.	Firstfruits Long Forgotten	29
21.	Autumn Is a Greek Sea	30
22.	Greece Fell Long Before the Sun	31
23.	Rome Sets on the Sun	32
24.	Roman Pastoral	33
25.	Columns of Rome	34
26.	Portia, My Love	35
27.	Mother of Tears	36
28.	Roman Peace	37
29.	Sunset over Black Pearls	38
30.	Roman Street Boy	40
31.	Because Stones Do Not Pray	41
32.	The Going Blind of Rome	42
33.	Bone-Lipped Love	44
34.	The Weighing of the Heart	45

35. She Was Made from Antiquity and Storm	46
36. Seduction by Many Roads	48
37. The Sicilian Peasant Girl to Her Love	49
38. The Lost Wellspring of Voice	50
39. Poem of Sicily	51
40. The Plowman of the Alone	52
41. The Old Painter of Sicily	53
42. Empire of Peasants	55

Mediterraneo

43. To the Sky	58
44. My Mother, the Sea	62
45. Waters of Rebirth	65
46. Like the Medieval Snow Melts	67
47. Here Hang the Wine-Sotted Troubadours	69
48. Two Truths of the Snowflake... and a Lie	71
49. Lion of the Hills	73
50. The Great Mortality, or the Modern Plague	74

Sparrows, Little Twitter Poems

51. Of Aesop and Sparrows	76
52. The Poet Outlives the Muse	77
53. Bird with the Little Eye	78

54.	Death Is a Fluttering Bird	79
55.	The Library of Sunlight	80
56.	Bookmark	81
57.	The Lit Fuse	82
58.	Things Lost and Looked Away	83
59.	Aubade for a Forgotten Lover	84
60.	The Death of Mozart	85
61.	Viennese Dark Chocolate Cake	87
62.	Here Be Dragons	88
63.	Watermelon Dusk	89
64.	The Old Sailor Dreams of Mermaids	90
65.	Algonquian Love Song	91
66.	Bridge of the Snowflake	93
67.	Angel Tongues	94
68.	Every Flower	95
69.	Hiroshima Survivor Tree	96
70.	Garden of Forever Weeping	97
71.	The Dragon of Snow and Starlight	98
72.	Powdered Tears	99
73.	To Our Love That Never Was	100
74.	The Light from the End of Eternity	101

75. What I Will Miss	102
References	103
About the Author	105

~ To my parents, Joe and Pat, with all my love for your years of unending support and patience ~

Preface

This book of poems runs the gamut from antiquity to more modern musings. As such, I have separated the book into three parts, the first of which lends the title to the whole. While the focal point of this first part is undoubtedly a modern perspective on Ancient Greek and Roman culture, there is more than a passing glance at Mesopotamian, Egyptian, and other ancient civilizations, both real or imagined. It is difficult to seek the authentic voice of the Ancient Greeks and Romans, though I did at least endeavor to seek the authentic feeling of a distant time and place, through modern eyes as well as all eyes. I have tried to order these ancient poems chronologically and thematically but, wherever that posed a challenge, I simply placed the poem in what I considered its natural spot, hopefully for the better reading experience.

The second part, Mediterraneo, focuses on the still more modern sense of the Mediterranean and European world with the central theme of continual rebirth while embracing the past. Many of these poems have a shadow of a place in the first part, but I felt like they deserved a bit of distance to simmer in their own kind of shadowy starlight. I tried to group these poems more by theme than chronological order but still again in the interests of readability.

The final part, Sparrows, Little Twitter Poems, touches on some fleeting and some fancy work, much of which had no place in the first two parts. These are not lesser poems as much as they are less-than poems, not quite at the historical watermark of the two earlier parts. As such, some readers might even prefer them for their variety, simplicity, whimsy, or more modern style. I chose thematic grouping here as well, but placement of poems is one of the most difficult challenges in compiling a poetry book. I will leave it to the reader to decide if I accomplished that or indeed if the poems themselves have merit on their own.

Poems of Ancient Rome and Greece

Dancing Satyr Press

1

Ancient Roman Coin

Fall to me, all you streets of Rome,
    With your embrowned oils from torched walls and breccia of shadows,[1]
    The pizzicato of stairways and afternoon slowly closed[2]
    Like the thick, leathery-echo from this book of all roads.

    Fallen, smoldering empire of storefronts and back-shop heirlooms,
    Your lupine hills unbound with milk of cur in the wind and woods,
    To your fallow fields rowed deep by a conquest of oars,
    To the deepest silence and soot-muted oneness of Pompeii,
    And a sky that is an ancient coin, without worth,
    But still rubbed smooth at the edges by overfond lovers.

---

1. "Breccia" here conveys fragmented, stony shadows.

2. "Pizzicato" means a technique of playing with plucked strings.

2

Sunset Whispers to Itself

S unset whispers to itself
  ~ No time outlives Time ~

The meltemi winds crackle the wild millet,[1]
Graze-feed upon the stalks of Greek plains,
The pelican scoops up the honeyed Aegean,
Waves of sunlit anise and almond in refrain,
Vestigial as the sweet persimmon from Egypt,
The hammered warmth from the flat anvil of Africa,

Sunset whispers to itself
~ No time outlives Time ~

---

1. "Meltemi" are the dry northern winds that blow across the Aegean in summer.

3
Egyptian Bird

The desert is a hummingbird
  With wings of hovering heat
~ Weightless idler ~
Forever in love with the acanthus leaf
And the nectar of the far Aegean.

4
The Sumerian Goddess Grows Old

Love not the empress curve of your cheek,
The many-storied, empty ziggurat of belief,[1]
The man-handled, baked brick built so high,
Your grotty thighs are pasted with all your lovers,[2]
Your lacquered heart is glazed by grief,
Head-bearer of broken vases as your crown,
Filled with dry dust from liquid stars.

---

1. The "ziggurat" is one of the earliest temple forms in a tiered structure like smaller successive boxes stacked on top of each other. This was first erected in Sumerian civilization and extended into other Mesopotamian civilizations like Babylon.

2. "Grotty" means dirty, squalid, or seedy.

5
Heart of Giza

Trace my love in the half-shell curve of a woman's back,
Like the naked wetland of Egypt, ibis-nest of the Nile delta.
Lovely woman, throw your arm back like a tethered cord,
To this sledge-mason for your pyramids, this falcon-doting ward
Of your gold capstones, all-seeing eyes over the west-bank shore.

Love, our days of polished limestone are wind-scoured,
Left like a pile of petrified fruit from figs and bottle gourds.
Love, always forget me, now the sand has filtered into my pores
And cascades into the empty shell of my quarried heart.

6
Babel Sighs in Ruin

A sigh is a barebacked rider, soundless along a sandy coast,
A candle tipped with starlight, wheeling in a cosmos of smoke,
A firefly floating on the ruins of the wind like a winged gyroscope,
A skull in the stomach whose teeth are my own and breathes
With Babel's thousand tongues telling fragrant untruths.[1]

---

1. Babel and Babylon are synonymous, though the former is the original Hebrew variant and takes on an allegorical meaning in *Genesis* with the Tower of Babel, which humankind intended to build to the sky through one unified effort and language. In the parable, God confused their speech as punishment for their hubris and dispersed humanity across the world.

7

Winged Seeds of Babylon

The cicada husk of the crescent moon sheds in cyclides light,[1]
Molted whispers of life, spread like perfume behind the ear,
Or like silver earrings unadorned and scattered around the night-lit table.
Here too, the garden gown of Babylon lies heaped in soiled ruin,
Beaten down to sand at the foot of the bed of the Tigris and Euphrates.

Though these sand dunes are its aerial, root-bound springs,
Though the underground nymphs tend with cicala wings,[2]
And underspurt of incessant summer song to lure

---

1. "Cyclides" are geometric shapes, similar to earrings in form. This also can be read as a play on "Cyclades," the early pre-historic civilization of islands in the Aegean, in the sense that all cultures shed down their own light and wisdom.

2. Almost all cicadas (also called cicalas), including periodical cicadas, live primarily as underground nymphs until they emerge above ground in the adult form for several weeks to months.

The resurrection rose of Jericho to bud once more,[3]
In desert-faith for the hanging garden of a full moon.

---

3. The resurrection rose or rose of Jericho is the name for two varieties of resurrection plants, one of which grows in Iraq (modern-day Babylon). The hardy plants can survive extended droughts and, like the Biblical city of Jericho from which they take their name, are thought to be reborn from ash.

8

My Love Looks Too Far into Me

Her eyes are the lighthouse of the Pharos,[1]
Alexandrian, bronze-mirrored fire flung round
The gloaming coastal sorrow like sand-glittered spears.

Her praying mantis limbs of light,
Sever-poised for needlepoint strike
At the jeweled glint of wings in dim, rare-seen limits,
Now one with her rasping sea of scarab beetle husks.

---

1. The Lighthouse of Alexandria (c. 280 BC) was one of the seven wonders of the Ancient World. It was also called the Pharos of Alexandria because it was situated on the island of Pharos.

9
Undercurrent

Her memory is like the beauty of the silted Nile,
Of sacred blue lilies and heron
And skimming eyes of the crocodile.

10
Love Is a Phoenician Breeze

Love is a Phoenician breeze,
Purest abjad of Tyrian purple and royal blue,[1]
Pillow bearer of golden consonance between kings.

Love is a Phoenician trader over deepest-sounded seas,
Farthest-blown nomad that still wants for the thunder of golden drums
And the rain that comes in rounded vowels of water.

Because love has no tribe but is the purest nomad.

---

1. "Abjad" refers to the Phoenician alphabet that had only consonants and no vowels. It is considered a pure abjad and was one of the first alphabets spread through the Mediterranean.

11

The Desert Is Not a Grave

The desert is not the grave of the sea.

***

The heaving reign of pharaohed seas,
Rule in bloodline of palm wine and embalming fluid of brine.[1]
The tides are their mummified lips,
Whispering the coming forth of spells eternally to the sky.[2]
All goddesses, like shawled Isis, in lamentations of hair
And past-wept somnolence for Egypt,
Lie across the heart-bound murmur of waters
From their dead kings and the kingly divine, Amun-Ra,[3]

---

1. "Palm wine" and spices were used to rinse out the abdomen of the remains of the dead body.

2. The Egyptian Book of the Dead was a phrase coined in the 19th century. A more literal translation is The Book of Coming Forth by Day or Spells for Going Forth by Day.

3. "Amun-Ra" is the supreme god of Ancient Egyptian culture, combining the earlier gods of Amun (king of gods) and Ra (the sun God).

Whose bird-starred eyes fill the canopic jar of the cosmos.[4]

***

The sea is the grave of the desert.

---

[4]. The heart was actually the only organ left intact in the mummified dead. The other organs were kept in canopic jars though some were re-bound and reinserted into the mummified remains.

12

Sea of the Parthenon

Marble made of seagulls' wings, set in flight,
Their beaks foam and crest and rise for air,
In headwinds and feathered drag, upward lift,
Carve out fluted columns by tunneling vortex,
Beams of bluebirds made from cross-sky stitch,
Parthenon of flying tides and nested Acropolis,
Endless fossilized sigh of Saronic Gulf sea-winds.[1]

---

1. The "Saronic Gulf" is part of the Aegean Sea, west of Athens and encompassing its chief port, Piraeus.

13

The Histories

So Herodotus muttered marble dust into his beard,
And foretold the white clay of the mule road,
And the whiskers of Greece grew long with legend.[1]

---

1. The Histories (c. 430 BC) of Herodotus are widely regarded as the cornerstone of historical works in Western Culture. Though it primarily documented the Greco-Persian Wars, the work's reliability has often been questioned, giving rise to the belief by some that it is a work of fable and legend rather than of chronological accuracy.

14

Summer War of Youth

Brother, our young summers held us in a long chain like the phalanx of bronzed soldiers forward flung,
And the lion was skinned and hung out to dry like the sunned-fur of the beach at Marathon.[1]
  Brother, help me to dream again.

Brother, our yellowed days shook us like serried Hoplites of an atomic age,[2]
  Shoulder to shoulder, friction rubbed, all ranks split from the fissioned-flanks.
  Brother, help me to dream again.

Storm-footed Titans of heat, dust, and irradiated wind pry from a ruptured Tartarus,
  The flanks are an open pulse; the scorch-song thirsts for its sea-cooling to stone.

---

1. A recounting of the Battle of Marathon during the first Greco-Persian Wars (c. 490 BC), a battle in which the Greeks triumphed by pushing the Persians back to their ships at sea.

2. "Serried" means to close ranks and stand shoulder to shoulder.

Brother, the lion lives that wears your skull around its mane.

Brother, dream of me again, of Persian arrows and lances,
And my fallen eyes instead of yours pouring in
With a sea of lavender water and mists
And summers of once-were.

15

Heroic

The Trojan dead are whispering
   Indecipherable secrets to sodden-eared earth.
The wind has eyes and sees beyond, Titans outremembered.
Ajax and his oft-turned back
Carries again the fallen from the fields:[1]
    The murder-slept clouds, unsuspecting,
    Slumped Achilles of disbelieving-godless eyes,[2]
    Flinging the final spear of his own blood,
    Soldiers all now of the green husk.
Titanic silence engulfs sound,
Except from those who mourn.
The storm is only a storm
As long as the leaves are lost.

---

1. Though there are many variants to the myth, Ajax who was known as much of a warrior as Achilles, in many of these tales carries Achilles' body from the field in a show of honor.

2. In the post-Iliad Homeric world, Achilles was struck in the heel by an arrow shot from Paris, brother of Hector, whom Achilles had defeated in battle during the Trojan War. Achilles died as a result. Achilles' mother had dipped him in the river Styx as a baby, holding him by the heel, to make him invincible except at that precise point where she held him.

Such is the untimely, timeliness of war.

16

Omens of the Oracle

Like the frog of batrachian notes in the inkwell of swamp,[1]
And the bee waggling hieroglyphs to the papyrus of hive,
Like the flight of birds in the palm of radiating skyline,
And the sad might of the world to the caged dog's eye.

---

1. "Batrachian" here means frog-like and also alludes to "Batrachomyomachia," the epic parody of The Battle of the Frogs and the Mice, misattributed to Homer.

17

Apollo of Wolves

B low, Lyceum grasses, blow,
From coiled lips of your wolf-god Apollo[1]
Whose dawn-padded paws to starprints roam
This temple-tribute to thought-illumined roads.

Blow, Lyceum grasses, blow,
Of wave upon wave of your brushings-by,
From staff to sandal-fall to cloak hemline,
For rhapsodes, your song-odyssey to sew.[2]

The Greeks built the sun,
Upon scaffolding ~ *acrobaticon* ~[3]
With pear-skinned lightness to glow,
Or like leavened bread from the woodburning stove.

---

1. The Lyceum, known for Aristotle's peripatetic school (or walking school of thought), served as a temple dedicated to Apollo, who has been known as the God of Light, Poetry, and Wolves, among many other things.

2. "Rhapsodes" were verse singers, or stitched-song singers, in the Lyceum and Ancient Greece. Scholars believe Homer's works were sung this way.

3. "Acrobaticon" means Greek scaffolding.

Blow, Lyceum grasses, blow,
The sun lies old on its famine-cracked pillow,
In spittle of gold and yellowed phosphorous,
With the gods past-blown to ruin.

18

Oblivion Conquers Us

Keep your trees, keep them for your heaven of ashen dusk
And night like the pale-faced deathmask of emperors,
No reason that the commoner to oblivion is hushed,
These old-wise woods and leaves, peopled without us.

Keep Macedonian dust lightly conquered over the breeze,
So that it shoots its tail like the centuries-sole comet,
The scorched earth left by Alexander's mapmaker eyes,
Swung wide like his *Sarissophoroi* over Persian might.[1]

Remember the lesser grove of his teacher Aristotle's tribe,[2]
They have only slipped their sandals off, to bare themselves
Of sound and the concourse of the foot's impulse,
Caught the lithesome wind, to flow outside our hearing,
And muse as empire of air and loss and forgotten walks.

Keep your trees and the darkening sky through them

---

1. "Sarissophoroi" were Macedonian light cavalry under Alexander, so named for the pikes they carried (sarissa).

2. Aristotle taught Alexander until his mid-teens.

That remind me of the passing into the past.
Never is the poem from tongue of blade or plow.

19

Love Lost in Every Sky

Love, unruliest hope, when fierce Diana went wild
With savage discourse, the arrow-stroke of her tongue—
While rage-hounds bay in wooded Gargaphie—aimed at Actaeon.[1]

Or old Baucis her god-giving bone fat of mind,
Stewed the broth of covenant for Zeus to repay in kind.[2]

Then Parthenope, siren-stung in her whirlpool of sea vines,
Her maiden-voice was a breath of sand for Naples to nurse from.[3]

The body of Helen still lies in ages-old smoke over our cities,

---

1. Diana, goddess of the hunt, turned Actaeon into a stag who was then chased and killed by his own hounds; he had gazed on her bathing in her sacred wooded valley of Gargaphie.

2. Baucis and Philemon, an old couple, provided food and shelter to two wandering peasants, the gods Zeus and Hermes in disguise. The town had shunned the two, and Zeus urged the old couple to safety while he destroyed the town. Their home then became a temple.

3. Parthenope, a siren whose name means maiden-voice, drowned herself when she failed to lure Odysseus; her body washed up on the shore of what became Naples.

We live in the timberframe of her bones of burned ships.[4]
Why can't her death be an end to all skies?[5]

---

[4]. The well-known myth of Helen, whether seduced or abducted by Paris, launched the Trojan War and as Christopher Marlowe famously wrote, "Was this the face that launch'd a thousand ships, / And burnt the topless towers of Ilium."

[5]. All these myths have some form of love, whether unrequited, holy, self-sustaining, or ruinous.

20

Firstfruits Long Forgotten

Sings a small boy whose hair is tousled by the wind,
As too the folds of his mother's peplos and the robes of clouds,
When Greece gathers in silence like the stillness for a deposed crown,
And all Athens around, the song of *Eiresione* for firstfruits of Autumn,[1]
Singing boys with the olive branches of colored wool and garlanded gourds,
A fall-bird to wander the Ionic sky, foretelling of new sunrise.

***

How that joyful ancient voice still haunts the songbird of sunset.

---

1. "Eiresione" was an Ancient Greek song associated with a fall festival that some maintain was a precursor to Christmas. Boys traditionally carried olive branches with colored wool and sometimes hung with jars of honey, fruits, and gourds. The branches were then left by boys on individual doors as a token of good will and prosperity.

21

Autumn Is a Greek Sea

Autumn is a Greek sea,
A summation of wet leaves,
Gathered wicks of sunset,
A hypocaust of warm water,[1]
That lies beneath our feet,
Incense from the Sea of Crete,
Risen to the airy suggestive.

***

Autumn is a word in the mind, fallen leaf-like to the mouth,
How like the orange rind, our ancient past is shriveled under pillars.

---

1. "Hypocaust" was a hollow space under the floor where a furnace then supplied heat to homes, a central heating system that some references date back to Ancient Greece but certainly prevalent in Ancient Rome.

22

Greece Fell Long Before the Sun

A knife cuts clean the jugular of Greece,
Sun-shattered Autumn spurts in breezes,
Her face falls like crumpled sails of the trireme[1]
~ This is the sound of sinking clouds, mammatus ~
The slow tottering head sinks into itself,
The arm of once-command lies lengthwise
Next to the sea, as waves erase all her form,
And the drear and maddened moon in its cage of stars.

---

1. "Trireme" was a Greek galley ship of war propelled by three banks of oars.

23

Rome Sets on the Sun

Rome has set on the sun,
   Spreads the rays of its streets
And the warmth of its torches.
Caesar commands nightfall come,
To make florid incense and wine
And talk as one full of the moon.

24

Roman Pastoral

Fall is an empty street in Rome,
 Of byways of dry-leaf stone and moth-haunted hours,
Of market stalls with their over-haggled and fingered rinds,
And melons moiled over and palmed and bruised.[1]
The light blows like once-told ripeness from the basket of fruit.

---

1. "Moiled" here means to struggle over or aggressively barter.

25

Columns of Rome

Every Autumn, the sky a little more to stone belongs,
The immovable strata of deciduous columnar clouds,
Every leaf that falls, Rome a little more to earth's heart recalls.

26

Portia, My Love

I make my grave in her dark treason of hair,
Fragrant master of soldiers and memories,
Bei capelli, conspiracy of internecine curls.[1]
Her upbraidings strangle all my sweet nothings
To breathless wish of the emperor-purple of lips.

Flow then like black gloss of birds
And the brood hatchlings of shadow, exiled eastward,
Fled like a premonition of warmth somewhere far off,
While the wine-colored blood spills Caesar's heart into a throng
of mouths.

Love, you are the hardest grave,
Were you ever just a kiss
Or always from daggers made?[2]

---

1. "Bei capelli" is translated from the Italian as "beautiful hair."

2. Porcia or Portia was second wife to Marcus Junius Brutus. She has been speculated to be one of the few who knew of the plot against Caesar.

27

Mother of Tears

When she folds into me and weeps,
    The world of empty things falls into me
Like the wetness of July in antiquated Rome,
Mother of Tears, *Mater Lachrymarum*, in Forum stone,[1]
The rain-addled veneers of Octavia's Portico.[2]

Gather up these black sickened bellies of ruins,
Turn them out to make hunger the den of the skies,
Let the cracked whisper of each monument and temple
Cease as Caesar, in unending stillness like a bare road.

A road is the sadness of seeing our beginning
But knowing love its far-off end is foretold.

---

1. "Mater Lachrymarum," is the Latin for Mother of Tears.

2. Octavia was the sister of Augustus, first Emperor of Rome and successor to Julius Caesar. She was known for her maternal bearing, devotion, and regal bearing. She was much revered by her death (c. 11 BC), and Emperor Augustus named the Porticus Octaviae in the Forum after her.

28

Roman Peace

Her dark hair falls like the lowered trumpets,
Soundless as the eyelid-close of Accursed Gates,[1]
Past the city's outer walls and alley-clotted throes,[2]
Some shield-hearted soldier sent to his earthen fold,
Her blood-rimmed sky-lids of night foretell the phantom peace
Of Autumn like a head sinking down with the fell-purpled leaf
of war.

***

Love, you once guided the black looms of Autumn,
Olive-skinned druid, you are a dark everything,
And a toss of your hair flings to dust all of Rome.

---

1. The "Accursed Gates" were the gates beside the Triumphal Gates in ancient Rome. For everyday use, the populace entered through the Accursed Gates (the opposite was an ill-omen) and exited through the Triumphal Gates. For triumphs, the army entered through the Triumphal Gates. For funerals, the way was reversed and the dead exited through the Accursed Gates.

2. The dead were buried outside the city, the land of living.

29

Sunset over Black Pearls

The ancient way across this world lies like sunset over black pearls.

The treetops are marble-made that the riffler of wind deforms,
To know all mother tongues from the quarry of rough stones,
To speak everything at once, Bride of Unbecoming,
The moldering walls of lips, the kiss of vacant streets
And the quiet, wet solitude bespoken by back roads,
The whispered origami of the Forum, paper gods in folds,
Smothered in the false pillows of their own repose,
The wolf's beard dipped in its fresh pant of dewfall,
While lovers have placed on the stones of the Appian Way
Their perfect hearts like votive candles, cupping the flames,
Looking down the swift arrow of loneliness, Sagittarius its same
Heaven-glow and besprinkled guidepost of a starlit Sacred Way.
Mother of Rome, your powdered face has been made into bone by those
Unreturned home, your far-off travels lead only to the graves of sons.

The ancient way across this world lies like sunset over black pearls.

30

Roman Street Boy

The dead lie like Rome,
   Like toppled sunshine in stone,
From a boy who had blown
Into the seashell of the Forum,
Heard back in sound re-stoning, the alley of home,
The narrow basket-flowered *angiportum*...[1]
But, lips too strong, let out unknown
The stone-witherings of Medusa
And the bone dust of empire.

---

1. "Angiportum" is Latin for narrow street or alley.

31

Because Stones Do Not Pray

Because stones do not pray, even in their centuries' quiet,
Because the vines are long, only for the sake of length,
Not like the drab Orpheus-song that always up-ruins.
Because vestal Autumn is a bride of noon-time rain,
A faithful stream with her white mist of suffibulum,[1]
Beside the path whose footprints are half-notes from the grave.

---

1. "Suffibulum" was the veil worn by the Vestal Virgins.

32

The Going Blind of Rome

The elucubrations of the lute, pulsing from the finger strums of starlight,[1]

Plum-twilight of the Colosseum like an emperor's bowl of plucked fruit,

As the night's ghost-gods are tuned to Castel Sant'Angelo, Hadrian's tomb,[2]

Who drink the dwindling hours from the wine-stemmed glass of musical moon.

But come the times out of tune, the dwindling of stone is the going blind of Rome:

Rome is built upon millions of eyes closed with the undersides of their lids tattooed,

---

1. "Elucubrations" here means night compositions or writing/composing at night.

2. The Ancient Romans believed in the "Di Manes" or "Manes," the collective soul of the dead that had been deified. Gravestones were often inscribed with Dis Manibus Sacrum, shortened to D.M., to acknowledge the spirits of the dead or these "ghost-gods." Hadrian's tomb (c. 139 AD) is possibly one of the most well-known mausoleums in the world, and one can imagine the ghost-gods converging here on a windy Roman night.

With labyrinthine aqueducts, far-aging roads, and traceries of Nero's Golden Home.

Then death its sight-sun blooms through, death the architect of Seven Hills renews.

33

Bone-Lipped Love

So falls Greece, so falls Rome,
And in their bone-lipped tombs
Forever those still listening for love.

34

The Weighing of the Heart

If I could love, I would take the best of marble and dove,
And craft her eyes like inlaid tombs in stone skyward flight.
Just so, the Egyptian khamsin wind, by way of Rhodes,
Alights with evenness on the trullo stone of Alberobello.[1]
Just so, the weighing of the heart lies between marble and dove.[2]

---

1. The "khamsin" wind is a hot, often sand-filled Egyptian wind from the south or southeast that can blow from March through May. The "trullo," or trulli in plural form, is a small round stone house with a cone-shaped roof, found in the Apulia region of southern Italy.

2. The weighing of the heart was part of the final judgment in the Egyptian journey to the afterlife where one's deeds were weighed in perfect balance against the feather of the goddess Maat to determine if life had been honorable.

35

She Was Made from Antiquity and Storm

She walked out of the watercolor storm of a fresco
Like a cowl-bound form in a light drizzle of rain,
Her mosaic tiles of ancient lovers' eyes, ceramic-borne,
Just as her hips held the curves of the urn ~ kiln-fired ~
The coiled heat of Greece still stinging through her flesh.

For her, the treetops had been the summoners of storm,
In kind, she flung down the wet grove of her hair, electral,
Pantheress of humid breath and fanged flair of lightning,
Tamed once in the cloudy cage of Pentelic marble of the Parthenon.[1]

But the world piled dust before her, baiting with its groveled roads,
For her black mullings, much-tasted rain, and heaven's leaves to fall.
If only the Michelango-to-come had carved the clouds of her

---

1. "Pentelic" marble is the white marble of Athens, notably the Acropolis, found in quarries near Mount Pentelicus.

For the light to remain, shining its centuries,
Then maybe the thunder would have been left undone.

36

Seduction by Many Roads

Love is a thousand women who fail to amount to one,
Peasant seductress with bared shoulders of red dun-colored roads and candle smoke,
Who pours down her wet, ungoverned hair, like a fast-fading storm to dry over Aurelian Walls,[1]
In that dark sneer of sultriness over the sentry-like stillness of ramparts and stone,
A wasp in water whose sibilance comes from what the sting makes,
Like the upgathered phalanx of spears in the sand,
Or the sisters of fate who have coiled their hair as sunset snakes,[2]
Her fingertips prick into me like much-traveled and ancient rain.

---

1. This refers to the famed Aurelian Walls surrounding Rome (c. 275 AD), which encompassed the much earlier Servian Wall (c. 378 BC).

2. The three sisters of fate, known as Moirai to the Greeks and Parcae to the Romans.

37

The Sicilian Peasant Girl to Her Love

The earth-dark octaves of her singing hair,
   Sung-circles of campagna, the citadel,
And campanile bells in the Segestano air.
The pail sits like an expectant kiss on the lip of the well.

38

The Lost Wellspring of Voice

I remember the hidden chapel bells in her voice,
The little cloister of her abbey looks that opened
To a lovelorn courtyard of cisterns and well works,
The sounding pulleys and ropes from the springs,
I will miss her nothing said to my infinite misgivings.

39

Poem of Sicily

Sicily is the golden caesura of history,[1]
Where the human poem is paused to hear
The exalted precipice of its own sigh.

---

1. A "caesura" is a pause or rest in the middle of a poetic line, typically indicated by punctuation; it dates back to Greek verse.

40

The Plowman of the Alone

These clouds of Italy are grown on vines,
    Infidels of skies, fruit bearers of wine-veined
Marble, fertile in spite of its own lifeless tableau,
Here thrives the succulent garden of the alone,
Where turns aside the burnt nape of the plowman,
Voyager of the cool midnight seas of the mind,
Up to this arable vine of sighs from outworn gods,
And hears his heart once more give up its throne.

41

The Old Painter of Sicily

A vintner of aged leaves in the wine-press of the sun,
Thin-skinned like the lucent grapes from the vine-runs
Of the island trellises and teal-cordoned waves, lowest slung
Fruit-laden bough of sky, Sicily, whose ateliers of rolled cigarettes[1]
And uprolled sleeves like tides tease smoke into studio paints,
The black apple wine of storm made into mouthfuls of pulp rain,
Before the sunrise is gathered again in fishing nets and crab pots,
The coastal towns with their salted roofs of pied clay and pigeons
Along the lava stone streets, and night from the chanteuse of Egypt,
Singing her coral to heron, as when her bird-like barefooted slaves
Left tracks across Old Kingdom wastes, so this dreaming old man
Leaves his wrinkles to these grapes and across the sand-island pillow,

---

1. "Atelier" is simply an artist's studio.

Asleep with his fathers, hay-hauling peasants of wandering darkness.

42

Empire of Peasants

Death is to become sunshine,
 To break open the self to the world,
In sunwheat gold and peasant hearth.
(The sun is the only empire of peasants)
Every grain of annihilation is still a seed,
And the sunlight carries the sleepless dead,
Their melted voices are warm upon our ears,
The sounds rooted in, but when we do not hear,
No more than the dead worshiping the dead.

Mediterraneo

Dancing Satyr Press

43

To the Sky

Once more, comb your skiey streaks of hair,
    Backbrush to sombrous chamber,
While the vanity mirror flares its celestial impulse.

    The corner of the room is a privation like monastic air,
    Its angularity, the ascetic to your fleshened curves,
    More fitting for a candle fasting itself bare,
    Relinquishing shine to that spare resurrection in the panes.

    So too your summers have flamed upon the windows,
    And autumn has fizzled in spurts of leaves,
    So too the failed days are sublimely worshipping
    To a soul that is the glass between.

    Love is this placelessness of sunlight,
    Earth, the memento of where we touched once:
        Her haystack-gold of hair, his shy, straw whisper,
        And the footpath that still dwindles there to sunlight's pebbles.
        So warm is the insubstantial, substance of love.

From these paths, the world wanders old,
Upon its crooked staff of trees, its absent-mind dozed into hollows:
> No more sipping at Christ's wound,
> Like a glass soul filled with wine,
> Or tasting his body's amaranth
> In bee-breads fabled to divide.

Where lovers meet, death comes to adore.
Every kiss should prove monument to the world that wastes in air,
Every love should spurn its centuries to that steeped exile of elsewhere,
And break time like shells upon the shore.

II

Shut the blinds to the duller desuetudes of sun,[1]
Because evening itself is a falling in love,
Because moods are the seasons homespun,
And death's great measure, if it comes,
Will be padded upon hand-woven rugs.

So begins the conceit,
Spring its slippered caprice,
Subdued to the stairs, the down-turnings and creaks,

---

1. "Desuetude" means falling into disuse.

Until table-spread as the meadowed indulgence of the dining room,
   Where mornings have had their honeys,
   And the berries and creams were guilty pleasures past noon.

From the china closet and its glass goblet fruit,
Pluck the pome of a teacup[2]
And pour the brook of brews:
   Within the china pattern of leaves,
   The forest-dark shades of tea
   Are wheeling with subtle complexion
   Of black-currant and grey and darjeeling,
   As if the world could sway so wholly under the thumb,
   As if the woods were a coercion of vapors sapient
   Over their fire-flared stratums.

In mute, cupboarded moments,
To learn the only sound of the soul,
Is rain along the glassings of bay windows,
Is April too lightfelt to hold, only to lose.

Like a nightjar, startle through the storm whorls and raindrop leaves,
   Fluster from the ragged brink of Spring,
   To presage the distance in shady inklings.
   And so then sail to Summering,

---

2. "Pome" here conveys the fruit and a small apple-shaped object.

Dry until vaporous wings leave cooled tatters like clouded light:
    To dry the sodden absence of a lover,
    Feel your frayed fingers through his sky-blue sleeves.
    Loop the tassel of hair through the collar,
    As before the looms with an armful of yarns to weave.
    Once more the windfall of hair,
    Like smothered lightnings to the static mass of air,
    In strike-soundings, a confession to the cloth,
    For man to adorn what woman must bare.

Click the lampshade light, the yellowed Autumn of album leaves,
    Thinking back is your lying down to sleep.
    Fall is the seduction of the sky,
    An innuendo of slight denudings,
    To lure the human sun from its fleshened prime,
    Into leering lusters and willowy fingers to writhe.

Make your skyward sleep,
    Past the kitchen that keeps its silence of floors,
    A bare reminder of what the snows are for:
    Sleep is the only snowfall of the mind, heavy-worlded and pieced,
    Outlying the hushing deep of pines.

To the sky, great remnant of Greece,
    Which has of human lips their redness,
    But of love, still its thought to speak,
    Mouthing hollow as the wide-open world.

44

My Mother, the Sea

My mother the sea,
    She woke my sandy eyes,
Just to tell me she had to leave,
Draw past the markets where the fish are sun-dried,
Snarled by the coral-rough hands of divers deep.

My mother the sea,
She left her running tab
Of the grocer's choicest greens,
Thumbed the velamentous rinds and spiny *scarola*,[1]
Her xylem and phloem are the slow moving cruciferousness of a breeze.[2]

My mother the sea,
Charwoman of tides,
Who dips and delves upon her knees,

---

1. "Velamentous" means membranous or membrane-covering, here to suggest melon rinds. "Scarola" is the Italian word for escarole, a leafy endive often used in salads.

2. "Xylem" and "phloem" are the water and food transport systems of plants, respectively. "Cruciferousness" is here intended to convey succulent green leafiness.

Who scrubs her brothel-coves with chamber lye,
Cyprian mistress of the salt-stained sheets.

I have looked for you, mother,
A *scugnizzo* amid the striped awnings of the marketplace[3]
~ like sails to the sky ~
Where the fishmongers hawk their pride
Of conch, cavallo, and black sea bream.[4]

I have looked for you, mother,
Walked sun-forged along the boardwalk,
Amid the neon-mascara of signs,
Hand-in-hand with only the ladyfingers of salt and vinegar fries,
Toward the crisp syllabub of pebbles and sand.[5]

A beach is window-warmth spread free, cosmopolitan,
The longeur of eyes crushed in the glass-dust of cities.
And in the sputtering of the frosted spume of tides,
Held broken seashells in my hands like broken needles,
Heard the pump-click of the ventilator through your mask of sand.

---

3. "Scugnizzo" is the Italian for a Neapolitan street urchin.

4. "Cavallo" is the Italian for horse but also refers to the crevalle jack fish, a large fish from the horse mackerel family, from which it derives its name. It is also known as the black cavalli. "Cavallo" was assimilated into the English language by 17th century navigators.

5. "Syllabub" here refers to the frothy beach edge of sand and tide.

My mother the sea,

A naked convalescent,

Whose ever-turnings have taken

A turn for the worse.

Who will know her by her death, who but me?

45

Waters of Rebirth

Venezia, its musical key of brick and shade
    And the canals in rejoining polyphony
Sweeten the dour Church-ear.
From the impasto knife and loose brushwork,
A thumb-smear of waves and gently-bristled strife
Rise to assumption of the cloud-submerged bay,
Mural of cristallo, only-light without landscape,[1]
Made too from the winds of Murano,
Its clayed blowpipe of waterways molding
The lagoon of blown glass and bouquet of colored sea-shadows.

The Tiber lies on its side, like the lion and fox,[2]
Licking its paws at empire's dust,
A drifting gaze of water that already foresees

---

1. "Cristallo" is actually a term that means clear glass, or glass without impurities, and was invented around the time of the Renaissance. Titian revolutionized impasto, the thick layering of paint, and the style of painting that contained no landscape in his "Assumption of the Virgin" (c. 1515).

2. The lion and fox was a nickname for Cesare Borgia.

The swift-run northward to Romagna,[3]
Where the veined fur of the roe will succumb...
A ripple twitches like one dark claw of the Borgia...

The watercolors of the Arno are a fresco
On the wet plaster of the lips of Firenze, Tuscan fire-dream.
Or like the warring leg in curve of counterpoise,[4]
Sprung foot-forward to the daring world
And arm slung down in stone-victory
From this valley, too much like Elah,[5]
With taunting eyes turned from the Medici toward Rome.

---

3. "Romagna" was Borgia's intended conquest.

4. This references the famed Michelangelo David sculpture, which was originally situated in the Piazza della Signoria, later Palazzo Vecchio, so that David faced Rome, much like the Florentines stared down the larger Goliath of Rome not to mention the internal threat from the Medici.

5. "Elah" was the valley where the Israelites camped when David defeated Goliath.

46

Like the Medieval Snow Melts

The fallen leaves are the shrouds of hoof prints,
    The withers of breeze reined to time-kept trysts,
Gentilissimo, *Cavalieri di Corredo*, Italian knight[1]
Whose path by pure lover's look is made clean.

We go back, we go back to the sun caught by handfuls,
Like the Medieval snow melts into Grecian stream.

Gentle knight, to your galloping song of Winter:
The sweeping rush of grass and gathering refrain
Of bells surrounds the long sloping meadow of
The muzzle, snorting freedoms of wildflowers past,
Leaving its bosky thunderbrush of tail like distant[2]
Summer storms and the slackening rhythms of rain.

We go back, we go back to the sun caught by handfuls,

---

1. "Cavalieri di Corredo," or Cavalieri Addobbati, were the elite of Italian Medieval knights on horseback.

2. "Bosky" is bushy.

Like the Medieval snow melts into Grecian stream.

The volplaning bird plucks from fish-eyed shallows,[3]
A gargoyle perches on an organ key, ever sustaining,
A woman plays the lute from man's hollowed rib,
As the priests with sophistry sweep the dust off sin.

We go back, we go back to the sun caught by handfuls,
Like the Medieval snow melts into Grecian stream.
But the clock cannot turn its face from its tears.

---

3. "Volplaning" is the downward dive of a bird.

47

Here Hang the Wine-Sotted Troubadours

Here hang the wine-sotted troubadours of sadness and clouds,[1]

~ Having played serenas to paramours lipping at the cup of an evening bawd ~

Like tethered donkeys now with their packsong of pastorela and alba,[2]

No more musical mensurations of the Virgin Mary, *Cantigas de Santa Maria*,[3]

But slung over the railings of dawn-blotted taverns or courts of renown,

Here hang the wine-sotted troubadours of sadness and clouds,

---

1. The troubadour flourished in France during the Medieval Ages (c. 1100-1350), primarily traveling from court to court.

2. These are all song forms: the "serena" (evening song for a lover waiting to consummate his love), "alba" (dawn song of a lover), and "pastorela" (song of love from a knight to a shepherdess).

3. The "Cantigas de Santa Maria," the well-known "Canticles of Holy Mary," are 420 poems sung by troubadours, each mentioning the Virgin Mary.

Like drinking gourds, their stringed citherns dangle from their shoulders,[4]

Leaking the strummed honey-wine of sound like the retchings of the nearby sea.

---

4. "Citherns" are essentially the precursor to modern-day guitars.

48

Two Truths of the Snowflake... and a Lie

The snowflake is castellated cold,
   Of chill crenellations and turnings narrow.
Court of pie-powders and gray-skied brazier smoke,[1]
Of inner maze-work dimmed to murder holes,
Or the hooded machicolations from tower spire[2]
Of oily darkness and arrowslits of Greek fire.

***

The snowflake is a Medieval reliquary,
The frozen skull of rain and blood clear of sin,
Wind-captive with its prayer of quiet
On quietest lips, close to wine and sacrament.

---

1. "Piepowder" was essentially a Medieval vagabond trader, and the court was an ad-hoc justice system at town fairs or markets to mete out justice to assembled piepowders.

2. "Machicolations" were shielded openings at the top of the castle or tower through which defenders could drop molten combustibles, similar to Greek fire, on the attackers.

Or the chapel and its waxen paramours
Of incorrupt body and candlelight upon the moors.

***

The snowflake is the mighty frozen spark,
Fire-forged and ironwrought,
Under the eye of Hephaestus,[3]
Blacksmith of sorrow's wind.

---

3. The God of fire, Vulcan to the Romans, who is known for his endless work at his forge.

49

Lion of the Hills

Morning was sudden-made as an onwardness of hills,
   Meant for donning crusade in chainmail glistenings,
The sun visored in misty slats of cold steel,
To glimmer fusty through the godded grove,[1]
A holy sepulchre, earthly-dim to its rafters of oak,
Where the forest-fall of sunlight shed its rosework,
And a red-breasted bird, its song-flight of dappled gleam,
And in the meadow, where colorful whorled the tale of Saladin,
Wayside flowers shook beneath the destriers' cloth caparisons,
A sunny fullness of vales for the crusaders' forest-heartened lungs,
And when this furthering of sights was sunken from,
Still an onwardness of hills to Jaffa like steppingstones.[2]

---

1. "Fusty" here means dusty, damp, and dimly lit.

2. The Battle of Jaffa in 1192 effectively ended the Third Crusade when Richard the Lionheart's forces defeated Saladin's army after routing them at Arsuf, though they failed to recapture Jerusalem.

50

The Great Mortality, or the Modern Plague

From the first, the fluid-filled sacs of stars,
   The yolk of yellow lightning and oily rain,
  Then the placental storm, birth-giver of roads and oxen loads,
  Witch towers made from silk hair and the peasant sucklings of plague,
  Whelped there by the milk of the river Arno, by turns pacified or stern.

  The Dark Ages is a storm nesting in the sky, built by posthumous stares,
  Piece by piece, a raven's birth from eyes and saliva of roads and rivers.
  Of the woman who gave birth, the sway of leaves where once fell hair,
  Only her lips hover in the air of warm sun,
  Like a fountain in the bare palace courtyard
  Suspiring, flowing, extolling...[1]

---

1. "Suspiring" in this context means sighing or breathing.

Sparrows, Little Twitter Poems

Dancing Satyr Press

51

Of Aesop and Sparrows

The soul has as its sextant the ribs opened wide,
   The heart its compass in fluid circuitous diatribe,
When each to zone the geometry of Greek sky
With its powdery fabulism of centaurs and stars,
From Aesop's wine of words to the untimeliness
Of sundials to Charybdis's bloom of giant watery eyes.[1]

***

To know oceans by the dry riverbed of my pulse,
To scale only as high as the sparrow's tomb of my heart.

---

[1]. Charybdis is one of two sea monsters (Scylla being the other) in Greek mythology. Aesop relayed this myth as well.

52

The Poet Outlives the Muse

The only love I have known is the bird that lives in my ear,
    In the wind and cloud tunnel of long ago, with a hot salve
Of sunshine poured into the singing hole, the warm honey
Of wives' tales, the remedy of home against the world,
Though the song has since flown.

53

Bird with the Little Eye

You too will die,
   Bird with the little eye
That sits outside in the green holly.
We say our goodbyes,
You with your nodding head
And me with my sighs.

54

Death Is a Fluttering Bird

Death is a fluttering bird unnested from one mind
To bring its twigs and mud to the next, startled mind,
Where it dwells, Death and its brood, silence.

Death is the fractured self, once removed from the mothering mind

~ In journeyed sadness ~

To its own end, fully aware of the whole and of its own disrepair.

55

The Library of Sunlight

Books are like the sun's rays,
Still giving off fingertip warmth,
Though long cut off from the source.

***

Books are sunlight and Greek silence
Captured in glass firefly jars.

56
Bookmark

She placed the bookmark of her hand in my heart,
So many smoothed pages ago.

57

The Lit Fuse

The lit fuse of her lips touching off
A din in the black powdery night:
Illumined and immolated am I.

58

Things Lost and Looked Away

When a woman averts her eyes,
    I feel the snow has secrets to hide,
Or from the small crook of her arm,
I feel the warmth of buried sunset,
In the charm of a country steeple.

59

Aubade for a Forgotten Lover

The goddess of the spent moon skulks to her feathery bed of fiery dawn.

Wrens through the uplands wend the fence weft with piecemeal straw.

Lips painted like pomegranate groves, dashed with fructifying sweets.

A kiss is a far-off and warm opening of lips like the sun into forest gleams.[1]

---

1. The aubade is a traditional poetic form of dawn rising with the parting of two lovers.

60

The Death of Mozart

Autumn was an old Viennese street held up in sacrifice to the sky,
With burnt-song offerings that still see through the clouds, as they see through you.
His was cobbler craft of reed-winded flame for the foot in tune,
Amid the outsnuffed shopkeepers' lights and the candlesmoke of midnight hours,
Pulsing above the inner heart of the Ringstrasse
Of brass signs and paving stones, misted and mute.
His was the candelabra of wick-notes
Wanded through the windowed rooms of forested night.
His were those woods filled with doorways, bookcases, and stairs
And everything dim and warm with people, no longer there.

***

The winter sunlight played across the keyboard of crypted windows,
And in the muted under-roofs of ice and snow,
On one window, like a hand in whole rest,

The caramelized glass swallowed the flame-image of the stray redbird
And the black carriage wheels that passed.

In the long hallway of the Viennese flat,
One candle remained lit in the mouth of song.

61

Viennese Dark Chocolate Cake

The horse breathes in the city, the world of unrelenting pistons
And steam from the jingling harness, and the jangling windows
That reflect the bolting sparrows like fire arrows in the coming night.
Viennese darkness is like the smell of the chocolatier mixed with snow,
Sealed in a sachertorte with the alley-crack of the riding whip on coach,[1]
Viennese sunshine is like the baker's soul, rising on flashing coppers and tins.

---

1. "Sachertorte" is the famous Viennese dark chocolate cake.

62

Here Be Dragons

I failed to love round, but fallen flat,
My head slumps down, over an ancient map,
My eyes roll back, over the mappa mundi verge,
Where waterfalls purl, and the sea serpent-sleep lies curled.[1]

---

1. Mappa mundi are surviving Medieval maps of the world that often depicted sea monsters and dragons. In spite of a common belief, most educated Medieval classes did not think the earth was flat (known as the Flat Earth myth) nor did most scholars from the classic Greek period on. Similarly, no old world map contains the exact phrase "Here Be Dragons" to connote uncharted territories, though dragons and sea monsters often allegorically depicted the same.

63

Watermelon Dusk

My finest dusk was the watermelon kind,
   When bats skitted in the shortcomings of light,
And on a picnic bench in the cool June of outside,
I felt the dogwoods and pines and other apple-greens
Fidget with insects in the newness of night,
I felt the only grace was
The watermelon kind, and though the world was newly
Dying in its freshness, the pulp squirmed
From my bloated, gleaming lips like
Blubber split from a whale's side.

64

The Old Sailor Dreams of Mermaids

The scrimshaw of the air, the long whales-tooth of sunlight
   Etched with seafarer's care and his great wantonness for the sea,
   A kiss as light as the bottlenose dolphin cresting from the water,
   Then night undressed and falling down like sliding beads of watery stars
   From the wet coriaceous porpoise skin and a tail of silver fire.[1]

---

1. "Coriaceous" here means leather-like and rubbery.

65

Algonquian Love Song

Come home from eagle-throated distance,
The canoe-tip of the crescent moon scuds
Into the silted, mud-bed of heaven.
Her face-dream beside the pine trees
The mollusc of purpled *wampum* beads shining.[1]

Bury my hands, *metmge*, in the eagle's nest,[2]
Carry my feeling words to her on wings.
Let her mix roots, berries, clay,
and the feather of my hands
To paint her face with my words and these trees.[3]

Or let my hands ripple like flat-fish
Above the silt-bed of her slim stomach,

---

1. "Wampum" is well-known as the colorful beads made from whelk shells and later used as currency in trading with New World explorers. The Algonquian language has a tremendous number of dialects due to the geographically scattered tribes from Canada to the central and eastern United States. I relied on Strachey's 1624 compilation (reprinted in 1999) of the Virginia Powhatan dialect for this poem.

2. "Metmge" are hands.

3. Roots, berries, clay, and sometimes feathers were used for face paint.

Held there in radiant scaled warmth.
Lappihanne, the rapid water of our river heart,
Like an arrow that glides from the bow,
My people where the tide ebbs and flows.[4]

To us both, the dark, golden edge of woods whispers, *nouwmais*...[5]

And the water arrow will never land,

But carried in my eagle's hands,

I say *nouwmais*, my love, and pierce through all darkness

To the empty path made full with the ripples of all who have passed.

My *wopussouc*, swan of the woods, let us dive into the dark, golden sea[6]

Of forever in the hills.

---

4. "Lappihanne" was the basis for the word Rappahannock, which is also the name of the tribe known as the "people of the ebb and flow tide" and the river of the same name.

5. "Nouwmais" means "I love you."

6. "Wopussouc" is a swan.

66

Bridge of the Snowflake

A snowflake is when life and death
Touch lips ~ not to kiss ~
But to breathe unheard words
Into each other's hollowed mouths,
Like a dark, unending woodlands.

67

Angel Tongues

Alstroemeria, Southern-rooted watcher of the skies,[1]
Angel tongues of Peru, with your virgin-blushed annunciation
Or Incan-hued sacrificial fire.
So much like the moon tongues of all rivers in first frost or first harvest.

Like first love, first death is the truest form,
And blooms in scorn of all its many-mirrored rivers to come.

---

1. "Alstroemeria" is a genus of perennial South American plant, also known as the Peruvian lily or lily of the Incas.

68

Every Flower

Death is a flowering inward,
— the cleistogamy —[1]
Like lips to our own souls,
Drinking ourselves to florid nothing.

---

1. "Cleistogamy" here means the closing of flowers.

69

Hiroshima Survivor Tree

Love beneath the linden tree,
The blue touchpaper of fingers entwined,
And sunsets of ignis fatui,
The lightning wick of lips and the caroming atom,
That once held the faces,
All but sear and blast wind and howl of eyes,
All of love adrift.[1]

---

1. "Hibakujumoku" means survivor tree or A-bombed tree in Japanese. The linden tree, Tilia miqueliana, is one such tree in Hiroshima, and a Linden Tree Monument exists at the Hiroshima Peace Memorial.

70

Garden of Forever Weeping

Garden of Gethsemane, under your Mount of Olives,[1]
The green-pitted translucence of night, where Christ,
Seer-in-knowing, writhes at the split seed of fission,
Break of night into the morning blossoms of Hiroshima's ash,
Of mercurochrome and zinc oxides and the red snow of skin,
And his resurrection, forever once-again, in atomic flash,
The smells of honeysuckle and hay of manger,
And his breath of molten potash.

---

1. Gethsemane is the garden at the base of the Mount of Olives where Jesus suffered his agony before his arrest and crucifixion.

71

The Dragon of Snow and Starlight

In our love for the wind and all that passes,
  Each smote of self, a wisp of loss and absence,
  Like the snow pendulous slips over last grasses,
  In the glow of the lamppost and unholding fences:
  So too the thousand-grains of breath
  Blow through our bodies' incandescence,
  And in the starlit-smoke from the dragon's mouth
  On wings of filth swirl the bone-edge of death.

72

Powdered Tears

I never learned to weep
But ground my eyes down
On the griststone of a mill
Turned sadness into powder
Then choked on my own weaponized sorrow.

73

To Our Love That Never Was

We live in the sunshine of our broken loves,
    Where window curtains flow like pouring water from aqueducts.

    Sunlight is the memory of an old world, and we are just
    Watchmakers who labor at the trumpets of time
    As if to blow from the mouthpiece and unwind
    The second hands and derelict hours of our luminous grief.
    So shines the scintilla of frost that covers the ancient wheat,
    Snow falls like the listenings of lovers in the dark, and we are just
    Cartographers of snowflakes, mapmakers of frozen eyes,
    To radiate the parallelogram of her strands of hair across the sky.

    These and these and these
    Were never ours.

74

The Light from the End of Eternity

The light from the end of eternity
    Comes in through the window glass
Sits on the sill with the red Anthurium
In the stenciled orange Waterford vase
Centuries down and decades done
From the grassy light of the Lyceum.[1]

If the sun were to choose where to die,
It would falter over Pompeii,
And lie like a broken godhead
Or lava poured into the pottery cups of
The open-skied houses.

---

1. As noted in "Apollo of Wolves," the Lyceum was known for Aristotle's peripatetic school (or walking school of thought) and served as a temple dedicated to Apollo.

75

What I Will Miss

When I die, I will miss
    A woman's long hair in the wind,
Not a timeless thing, but a thing
Without concern for time,
The way Rome always reminds
Of Greece, and Greece reminds
Of salt air and vines.

References

While there is an inordinate amount of material on the Classical era available to modern scholars, some of it is contradictory and much of it is legacy material from scholars of the early to mid-20th century, not to mention Herodotus to Homer and all the original source material. That is not to discount newer works, just to establish that the "old reliables" are still here for a reason.

I tried not to refer to books no longer in print, but the Seyffert book in particular, first published in 1891, remains a vast, pithy resource and launching point for further studies. It can still be found in heavily used copies or via custom reproductions and remains one of those "unknown" finds that is essential.

Selected Sources

Hornblower, Simon, and Anthony Spawforth, editors. *The Oxford Classical Dictionary, The Ultimate Reference Work on the Classical World*. 3rd Ed. Revised, Oxford University Press, 2003.

Knowles, Elizabeth, ed. *The Oxford Dictionary of Phrase and Fable*. Oxford University Press, 2000.

Seyffert, Oskar. *A Dictionary of Classical Antiquities, Mythology, Religion, Literature, Art*. Edited by Henry Nettleship and J.E. Sandys, Meridian Books, 1958.

Strachey, William. *A Dictionary of Powhatan*. 1624 edition. Evolution Publishing & Manufacturing, 1999.

The Shorter Oxford English Dictionary, Volume I, A-M. Oxford University Press, 6th ed., 2007.

The Shorter Oxford English Dictionary, Volume II, N-Z. Oxford University Press, 6th, ed., 2007.

Wallis Budge, E.A. *The Egyptian Book of the Dead*. Edited by John Baldock, Sirius Publishing, 2024.

About the Author

Chris Saitta has been writing fiction and poetry since a young age and pursued his studies in English Language and Literature at the University of Virginia. He was fortunate to study under renowned historical fiction writer George Garrett, who was always an immense wealth of knowledge and support to all his student writers. After earning his Bachelor's degree, Chris earned his Master's degree in English Language and Literature at Hollins University. He has lived in Virginia for most of his life and continues to appreciate the gifts of his close-knit family, friends, and two dogs.

Printed in Great Britain
by Amazon

5641dd20-6eb0-4e88-b4a0-9636fbd70f14R01